FAST FORWARD

Castles
Through Time

Published in 2009 by The Rosen Publishing Group, Inc.
29 East 21st Street, New York, NY 10010

Created and produced by Nicholas Harris and Claire Aston, Orpheus Books Ltd

U.S. editor: Kara Murray
Illustrator: Peter Dennis *(Linda Rogers Associates)*
Consultant: Richard Platt

Library of Congress Cataloging-in-Publication Data

Harris, Nicholas.
Castles through time / Nicholas Harris.
p. cm. — (Fast forward)
Includes index.
ISBN 978-1-4358-2798-1 (library binding)
1. Castles—Juvenile literature. I. Title.
UG401.H37 2009
623'.109—dc22

2008031529

Printed and bound in China

FAST FORWARD

Castles
Through Time

illustrated by Peter Dennis

text by Nicholas Harris

PowerKiDS
press™

New York

Contents

Introduction

Imagine you are standing on a hilltop somewhere in Europe, thousands of years ago. Some farming people have gathered to make their home here. They have built simple shelters and a high fence all around their camp to protect it. As the years go by, other people come to live on the same hilltop. They put up stronger and stronger defenses, finally building a castle with thick stone walls. The new castle will live a long and eventful life...

The story told in this book is like a journey. It is not a journey you can make by plane, car or ship. In fact, you don't have to *go* anywhere at all. You are about to travel through time. With each turn of the page, the date moves forward a few days, years or centuries. You are still in the same place, but notice how many things change from one date to the next. Each date—each stop on your journey—is like a new chapter. The early forts, the building of the stone castle, the preparations to defend it, the siege, the rebuilding and fall to ruin—all tell the story of the castle.

Use the thumb index to travel through time! This will help you can make a quick comparison between one scene and another, even though some show events that took place many years apart. A little black arrow on the page points to the time of the scene illustrated on that page.

The Year 600 BC

Some farming people decide to build their village on a hilltop. The villagers' houses are round and made mostly of wood. Each has a cone-shaped framework of branches held up by posts driven into the ground. Bunches of reeds, called a thatch, form a roof, while dried mud or stone makes up the outside walls.

To protect their village, the people build up walls of earth called ramparts all round it. On top of the ramparts they erect wooden

Ditch

The entrance to the village, the gateway, is the most strongly defended part of all. Any attackers would have to climb the ramparts, cross the ditches, then face guards throwing spears down at them from behind palisades.

Building under construction

Gateway

Ramparts

fences called palisades. Safe inside the hill fort, the villagers tend their animals, cook food, chop wood, grind corn and weave cloth.

THE CELTS

The Celts, the first people to build a castle on this hilltop site, were a farming people from central Europe. Over the years they spread across Europe. They were divided into many separate tribes. They often fought one another for land. Besides being farmers, they were skilled metalworkers and active traders. As warriors, they were no match for the powerful Roman armies, who began to conquer most of their lands after 225 BC.

Grain store

Palisade

Ramparts

Thatched roof

Chariot

Cooking

Pigs

Weaving

600 BC

AD 100

1,000 years later

30 years later

10 years later

100 years later

A few weeks later

A few days later

100 years later

250 years later

250 years later

Today

7

The Roman fort had a thorn hedge all around it.

The Year AD 100

Ditch

Gateway

Barracks

Soldiers

Soldiers' quarters

Principia

Chapel

Courtyard

Stable

8

The Celts' hill fort was no defense against the mighty Romans. A Roman legion (group of soldiers) has quickly conquered the fort and built a new fort in its place. It has strong defenses, with ramparts built up from layers of dirt on the inside and stone walls on the outside. The walls are then plastered and finished with a brickwork pattern painted in red.

Inside the Roman fort are the soldiers' barracks. Their commander lives in a separate, much grander stone building. It has heated rooms and plenty of space for his family and servants. The fort's head-quarters is called the *principia*. A statue of the emperor is kept there. It is under guard at all times.

Gateway

Section of wall cut away

Bedroom

Commanding officer's house

Dining room

Courtyard

Kitchen

Ramparts

Stone walls

Entrance hall

Waiting room

Food store

Stable yard

600 BC

AD 100

1,000 years later

30 years later

10 years later

100 years later

A few weeks later

A few days later

100 years later

250 years later

250 years later

Today

9

The tower and palisade in a motte-and-bailey castle were plastered to make them look as if they were built of stone, rather than wood.

A Thousand Years Later...

The old Roman fort that once stood on top of this hill was deserted many centuries ago. People used the stone for building their own houses.

Now the Normans have arrived. The hilltop site is a perfect place for a new fort from which to rule over their lands. A Norman lord orders local people to build a large mound of earth called a motte. A wooden tower is built on the mound, surrounded by a high palisade. At the base of the motte is a courtyard, or bailey, where there is a hall, chapel, barn, stables, and other buildings. The bailey is also surrounded by a palisade and a ditch.

All the buildings are made of wood. They would easily be destroyed by fire, so the Normans plan to replace the fort with a stone castle one day.

The entrance to the castle is by drawbridge. If danger threatened, it would be quickly pulled up. But should the attackers gain entry, the defenders would hurry up to the motte, destroying the stairway behind them.

Hall

Stables

Gate

Drawbridge

Tower

Plastered palisade

Motte

Bailey

Grain store

Well

Chapel

Hay

Palisade

Ditch

FROM ROMANS TO NORMANS

The Romans' great empire lasted for many years, but it finally fell in the late fifth century AD. Germanic peoples from the east, whom the Romans called barbarians, conquered the western Roman empire. They settled in their new lands and set up their own kingdoms. One group, the Franks, ruled over the most powerful kingdom.

Another barbarian people conquered western Europe in the late 700s. These people were the Vikings, who came from Denmark, Sweden, and Norway. Many settled in the lands they conquered, including Britain and France. The Normans, descendants of the Vikings, were a powerful people from northern France.

600 BC

AD 100

1,000 years later

30 years later

10 years later

100 years later

A few weeks later

A few days later

100 years later

250 years later

250 years later

Today

11

Tools were made by the craftsmen themselves or by blacksmiths. Above left is a handsaw used by a carpenter. On the right are his axe, mallet, and chisel.

Thirty Years Later...

The hilltop site has been chosen by a powerful lord to be the place where his new castle home is to be built. The lord must have a strong, stone-built castle from which to rule over his surrounding lands.

About 1,000 men work on building the new castle. A master mason is in charge of the building work. He has a team of masons under him. Some cut and carve the stone (freemasons) while others build the walls (roughmasons). Carpenters make the wooden frame for the roof and build the scaffolding, wooden boards fixed to the walls that allow men to work high up on the new castle's walls. Blacksmiths make and repair tools.

Besides the craftsmen there are the laborers, workers who carry heavy loads and pull stones and logs up to the top of the castle. A treadwheel is a machine that helps with this task. As a man walks inside it, it turns, pulling on a thick rope with pincers on the end of it.

The thick castle walls are not made of solid stone. In between the outer layers of smooth, carved stone is a mass of rubble.

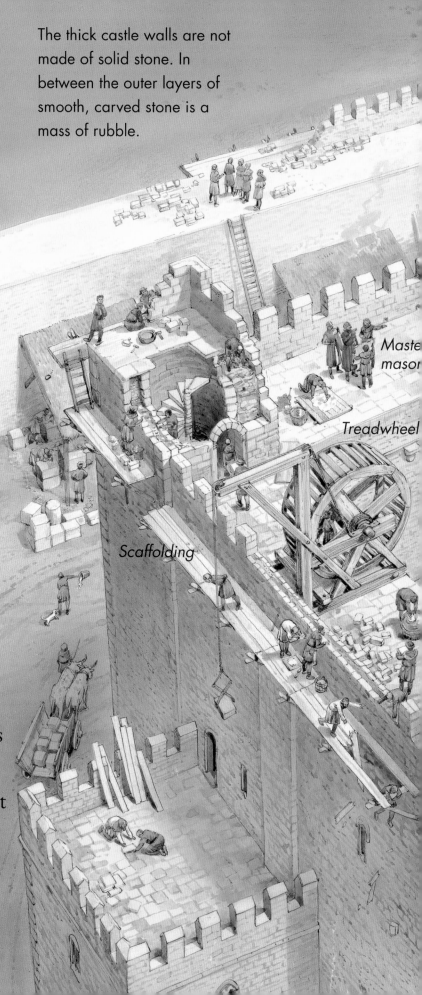

Master mason

Treadwheel

Scaffolding

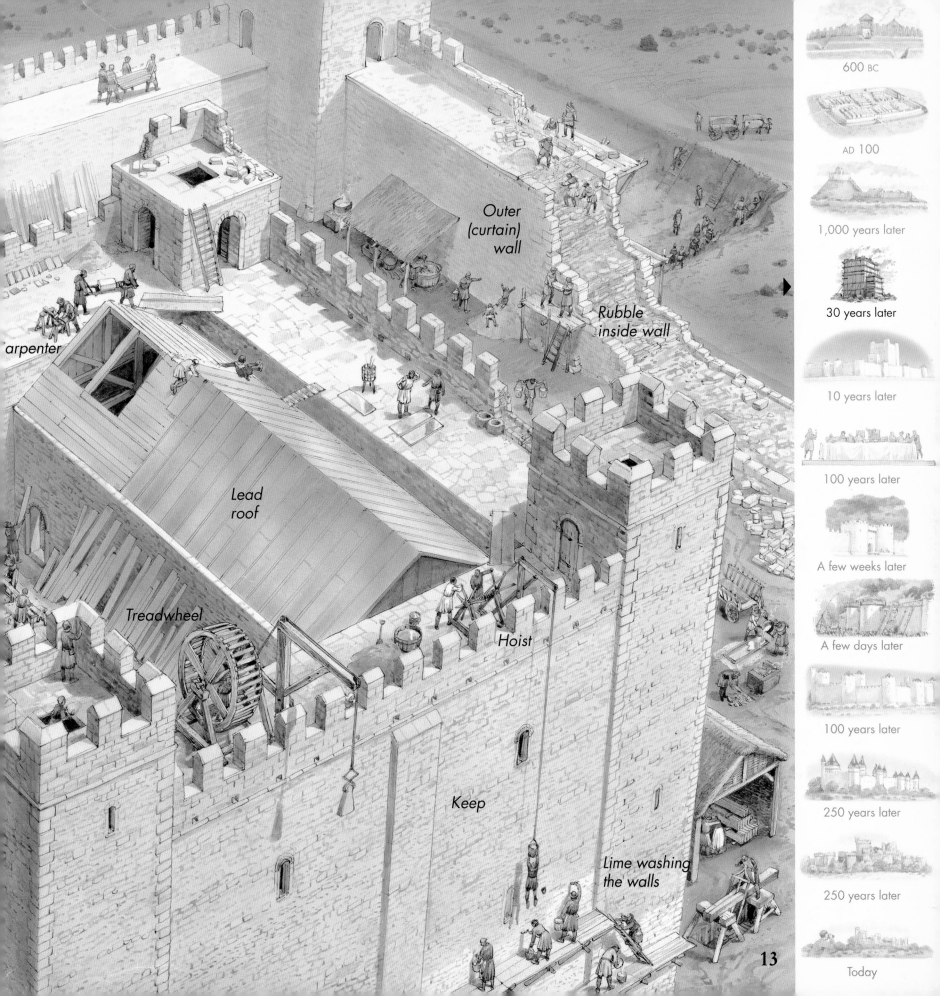

Outer
(curtain)
wall

Rubble
inside wall

Carpenter

Lead
roof

Treadwheel

Hoist

Keep

Lime washing
the walls

600 BC

AD 100

1,000 years later

30 years later

10 years later

100 years later

A few weeks later

A few days later

100 years later

250 years later

250 years later

Today

13

The castle was a home for the lord and his family. The lady took charge of the castle while the lord was away.

MIDDLE AGES

This period in history is known as the Middle Ages. In those days, the king gave land to his nobles (barons or lords) in return for their support in ruling the country. Noble families became powerful.

Keep

Bakery

Lord and lady

Pigsty

Stores

Well

Ten Years Later...

At last, the castle is complete. The magnificent stone keep, gleaming white in the sun, towers above the cottages gathered inside the walls. Delighted with their new home, the lord and lady set off on horseback for a day's falconry, accompanied by their favorite dogs.

Meanwhile, the castle is buzzing with activity. The steward checks the food store, freshwater is drawn from the well, and workers are hard at work in the kitchens preparing the meal for when the lord returns. A blacksmith makes shoes for one of the lord's horses. Up on the battlements, the guards keep watch.

Battlements

Blacksmith's forge

Kitchen

Hayloft

Stables

15

600 BC

AD 100

1,000 years later

30 years later

10 years later

100 years later

A few weeks later

A few days later

100 years later

250 years later

250 years later

Today

In the Middle Ages, falcons, birds of prey, were used as hunting animals. A falconer would wear a gauntlet, a glove to protect his hand, and carry a leash to prevent the birds from flying away.

Falconer

Taster

Lady

Lord

Cup-bearer

Steward (castle manager)

High table

Carver

Washing hands before meal

Floor strewn with sweet-scented herbs

Musicians
in gallery

Entertainers

A Hundred Years Later...

We are in the great hall. A grand banquet is in full swing in honor of the lord's guest, a neighboring baron. The two men have made an alliance, an agreement to help defend each other's lands in the event of war. It is time to celebrate!

The servants bring in the dishes. The first to be served are the lord and lady and their guests. They sit at the top table, which is covered with a linen tablecloth. They eat off gold and silver plates and drink from individual cups. The meat is carved at the lord's table and the best pieces are served to him and his honored guests.

The other diners sit at trestle tables. Their food is served up on dishes called messes. Each mess is shared between three or four people. They eat not from plates but from trenchers, pieces of stale bread that soak up the gravy (afterwards they will be given to the poor to eat). They share their drinks from jugs. Table manners are important—although not everyone cares about them!

17

600 BC

AD 100

1,000 years later

30 years later

10 years later

100 years later

A few weeks later

A few days later

100 years later

250 years later

250 years later

Today

A Few Weeks Later...

Most castles had spiral staircases (you can see one being built on page 12). They usually spiralled upward in a clockwise direction. This gave the advantage to the castle's defenders (provided they were right-handed) because it was easier for a swordsman to strike at an opponent standing lower on the stairs, who had to lean around the corner to use his sword.

The guards are in a hurry to prepare the castle's defenses. Another baron has found out that two of his rivals have formed an alliance. News has come that he means to destroy the castle.

The castle has impressive defenses. A deep ditch and a high wall several feet (m) thick run all around it. The castle gateway is especially strong. A drawbridge that crosses the ditch could be quickly raised up to block the entrance. Behind it are heavy gates and two portcullises, heavy gratings that slide down holes in the walls. Defenders could shoot arrows or drop stones down through "murder holes" on to the heads of attackers.

The castle's defenders build wooden hoardings around the battlements. From these, men could drop missiles on attackers standing close to the walls. Workers stretch wet hides over the hoardings to protect them from fire.

Preparations are nearly complete. Will the castle be strong enough to withstand enemy attack?

Building wooden hoardings

Outer (curtain) wall

Guardroom

Dungeon

Ditch

18

Gatehouse

Drawbridge winch

Portcullis

Murder holes

Gate

Drawbridge

Wet hides

A plan of the castle, showing
the position of the gatehouse.

Keep

Bailey

Gatehouse

19

600 BC

AD 100

1,000 years later

30 years later

10 years later

100 years later

A few weeks later

A few days later

100 years later

250 years later

250 years later

Today

A crossbowman loads a bolt into his weapon.

One way of breaking down a castle's walls was by undermining. Miners dug a tunnel beneath the walls, removing soil and rocks. The miners set fire to the wooden props that supported the tunnel and retreated. The tunnel caved in, bringing down the walls above it.

Wooden hoardings

Dead animal being slung by trebuchet

Drawbridge

Battering ram

Trebuchet

Ladder

Mangonel

Filled ditch

A Few Days Later...

The siege is under way. The enemy soldiers surround the castle and start to build the machines they need to attack the castle.

The soldiers fill in the ditch with stones and sticks. Now the belfry, a giant tower on wheels, can be rolled up close to the walls. Soldiers race up its ladder and leap over the battlements.

Meanwhile, crossbowmen and archers shoot their bolts, or flat-headed arrows, and arrows. Catapults pound the walls with missiles or fire flaming objects into the wooden hoardings. The giant trebuchet shoots rocks or the bodies of animals (or the heads of dead prisoners) into the castle, while the mangonel lobs small boulders. Other soldiers try to force their way through the gate using a battering ram, a tree trunk swung with great force from inside a wooden frame.

Soon the attacking soldiers force their way in. Fire rages through the building. Finally, the great stone castle will be completely destroyed...

Foot soldiers climb on to battlements

Belfry

AD 100

1,000 years later

30 years later

10 years later

100 years later

A few weeks later

A few days later

100 years later

250 years later

250 years later

Today

21

A Hundred Years Later...

After the siege, the castle was left in ruins. But it was not long before another lord decided to build a new castle in the same commanding hilltop position.

This castle is quite different from the earlier one. Although it still has thick, high walls and towers, there is no keep.

Knights were the most important fighting men of the Middle Ages. Skilled in fighting and horsemanship, they were also expected to be honorable and brave. The first knights wore chain-mail coats, made of thousands of metal rings tied together. By the 1400s, knights had switched to wearing suits of plate armor, which were more protective.

Watchtower

Bedroom

Chapel

Guard

Schoolroom

Brewery

Courtyar

Knight

All the main buildings are built inside the walls. They are more comfortable than the small, drafty keep. The round towers defend the castle. Inside them are extra rooms for guests.

Today, the lord is performing a dubbing ceremony. A young man is made a knight in this ceremony. The lord taps him on the shoulder with a sword, followed by a blow with the flat side of the blade.

Battlements

Bedroom

Great Hall

Dubbing ceremony

600 BC

AD 100

1,000 years later

30 years later

10 years later

100 years later

A few weeks later

A few days later

100 years later

250 years later

250 years later

Today

23

Two Hundred and Fifty Years Later...

This castle is at Saumur, in France. Like many French castles, or châteaux, it became a comfortable home for a wealthy family.

This castle was built during the nineteenth century for King Ludwig II of Bavaria, Germany. It was very unusual for a large castle to be built so long after the time of the Middle Ages, but Ludwig was fascinated by the days of knights and castles. He had the wealth to make his dream of a fairy-tale castle home come true.

Since it was rebuilt, this castle has not suffered any more attacks. The noble family who now live there can enjoy their home in peace. The openings for shooting arrows have been replaced by glass windows that let in more light. To the tops of the towers, no longer needed as lookout positions, tall, pointed roofs have been added.

Outer courtyard

Drawbridge

Gatehouse

24

FROM FORTRESS TO HOME

By the end of the Middle Ages, the power of the noble families had grown weaker. Kings and queens had taken greater control of their kingdoms. Battles between barons were now rare. Castles were, in any case, costly to build and much less useful as means of defense. For example, powerful cannons could blast great holes in the thickest walls. So fewer and fewer nobles built new castles, preferring to live in large houses instead. If a castle had remained unharmed, however, it could be turned into a comfortable home, living in a castle was the height of luxury.

Tower

Stables

Coach house

Outer (curtain) walls

600 BC

AD 100

1,000 years later

30 years later

10 years later

100 years later

A few weeks later

A few days later

100 years later

250 years later

250 years later

Today

25

Another 250 Years Later...

Since the Middle Ages, more and more powerful weapons were invented. Castle walls could now be blasted away by cannon fire. If, during a battle, an army tried to seek protection in a castle, it could not hold out for long. But few castles were totally destroyed. Some were harmed just enough so that they could never be used as strongholds again.

Even after a castle has crumbled to ruins, many of its original features can still be seen. These are arrow loops, narrow openings in the walls through which arrows were fired. From outside it was hard to shoot back through them.

The castle has fallen to ruin. The noble family that once lived there has moved away. Nobody has come to live in it since. The gardens have become overgrown. Tiles have fallen from the roofs. The weather has harmed the insides of the castle beyond repair. The gleaming white lime wash has flaked off the walls. Shrubs start to grow inside rooms left open to the skies.

Industrial town

Outer courtyard

Gatehouse

Drawbridge

26

Soon, people from nearby villages
visit the castle. It has all they need for
building or repairing their own homes.
They start to cut away at the walls and
take away stone, tiles and timbers.
Also visiting the castle are others
curious to discover how
people lived so many
hundreds of years ago.
Some find the ruins so
fascinating that they decide
to paint pictures of them.

Tower

Inner
Courtyard

Outer
(curtain)
walls

27

600 BC

AD 100

1,000 years later

30 years later

10 years later

100 years later

A few weeks later

A few days later

100 years later

250 years later

250 years later

Today

Today

The old castle has been undergoing repairs. Its walls have been rebuilt in places, to make sure there is no danger of them falling down. The trees and overgrown vegetation have all been cleared away and replaced by neat lawns and gravelled courtyards. Guardrails, steps, benches, information boards, and kiosks selling guidebooks and souvenirs have all been provided for visitors.

If you look around an old castle, it may be possible to find clues that tell you what the castle was like back in the Middle Ages. Here, for example, is an area of painted plaster. Now faded, it was once covered with bright patterns.

Can you see rows of square holes high up in the walls? These once held joists, long timbers that supported the wooden floors.

You may be able to see fireplaces all over the castle. Open fires were the only way to provide heat to castle rooms. Often, fireplaces can be found high up in the walls. They were once in rooms on higher floors whose floorboards have since disappeared.

Telescope

Tower

Brewery

School group

Kiosk

Ghost

Information board

People wander around the ruins, admiring the vast walls and towers. Some wonder what life would have been like for the castle occupants 700 years ago: where the lord and lady slept, what they ate at their banquets, or what happened when the castle was besieged. Of course, *you* only have to turn back through the pages of this book to find these things out for yourself!

CARING FOR RUINS

Many people now think that taking care of the ruins of ancient buildings such as castles is very worthwhile. If they were properly cared for, visitors would come to explore them and become interested in what life in a castle was like hundreds of years ago. Many castles all over the world have been carefully repaired and opened to the public.

Walkway

Chimney

Joist holes

Great hall

Inner courtyard

600 BC

AD 100

1,000 years later

30 years later

10 years later

100 years later

A few weeks later

A few days later

100 years later

250 years later

250 years later

Today

Glossary

arrow loops (ER-oh LOOPS) Narrow openings in castle walls through which arrows were fired.

bailey (BAY-lee) An open area enclosed by the castle walls.

battlements (BA-tel-ments) The jagged tops of castle walls.

belfry (BEL-free) A tower used by soldiers laying siege to a castle. As tall as the castle battlements, it was wheeled against the walls during an attack.

curtain wall (KUR-tun WOL) The outer wall of a castle.

drawbridge (DRO-brij) A bridge across a moat or ditch that could be lifted up to prevent entry to a castle.

gatehouse (GAYT-hows) A tower in the castle walls that hold the entrance to the castle. The gatehouse usually had extra defenses.

hill fort (HIL FORT) A stronghold built on a hilltop. Its buildings were surrounded by fences, ramparts and ditches.

hoardings (HOR-dingz) Wooden frames built on the outside of the battlements. They provided extra protection to the guards on top of the walls during sieges.

murder holes (MUR-der HOHLZ) Holes in the floor above the entrance to the gatehouse. They probably allowed guards to fire arrows or drop missiles on to enemy soldiers below.

palisades (pa-luh-SAYDZ) Fences built from wooden stakes used to protect an area or settlement.

portcullis (port-KUH-lus) A heavy wooden grating that could be slid down to close a gateway at the entrance of a castle.

ramparts (RAM-parts) Defensive mounds built around an area or settlement.

keep (KEEP) The main stone tower inside the castle walls. It housed the living quarters for the castle's residents.

legion (LEE-jen) A body of three to six thousand Roman soldiers.

lime wash (LYM WOSH) A mixture of lime and water used for painting the castle walls. It protected them from rain and made the castle gleam a brilliant white in the sun.

mangonel (MANG-guh-nel) A large catapult that fired rocks and missiles at a castle during a siege.

mason (MAY-sun) A builder in stone.

motte (MOT) A steep mound of earth on top of which a tower was built. A motte-and-bailey was an early type of castle.

siege (SEEJ) The surrounding of a castle by an enemy army to prevent supplies from entering it and anyone inside from leaving it.

trebuchet (treh-byuh-SHET) A giant catapult that tossed missiles such as rocks, dead animals or even human heads into a castle during an attack. It was powered with heavy weights.

Index

Web Sites

Due to the changing nature of Internet links, PowerKids Press has developed an online list of Web sites related to the subject of this book. This site is updated regularly. Please use this link to access the list: www.powerkidslinks.com/fastfor/castle/